I0419638

BATHS AND KITCHENS ON A HOUSE AND FLATS

A BOOKLET WRITTEN, DRANW AND PHOTOS TAKEN
BY

NOEMÍ MONTSERRAT GONZÁLEZ LÓPEZ

ARCHITECT

INDEX

1. PROLOGUE

The users of the buildings develope certain basical activities as cooking, eat or have a relaxing bath, this are realized in baths and kitchens.

Because of this, I dedicate that occasional paper that pretends give to the lector ideas or set a standard to companions, students, people who works in construction or even curious.

This zones should be sectorized, as example, the semi-public ones on day-living zones...the private where someone is going to sleep in case of baths, or another private function.

You can use some projectual methods to separate them as corridors or distributors on a well-designed house or flat.

Baths, kitchens and laundries, as we will see, can be private or semi-public. This ones obey in each case to the necesity of the project to give to the users a service reflexed on the architectural program.

PUBLIC ZONE	SEMI-PUBLIC ZONE	PRIVATE ZONE
Entrance-hall Living room	Bath-kitchen-laundry	Suitte on the second level

Figure 1. Zonification as a privacity degree.

It shouldn't cross the fluxes or circulations between them, derivated from the relation of the different zones or ambients and inter-ubications of each room.

Figure 2. Diagrams of circulations, depending on privacity.

It will be important take care of the way of door openings and the ubication of constituents of the bath and accessories or even the design of furniture on the kitchens.

Also, we should consider, as example, where are going to remain the heating units.

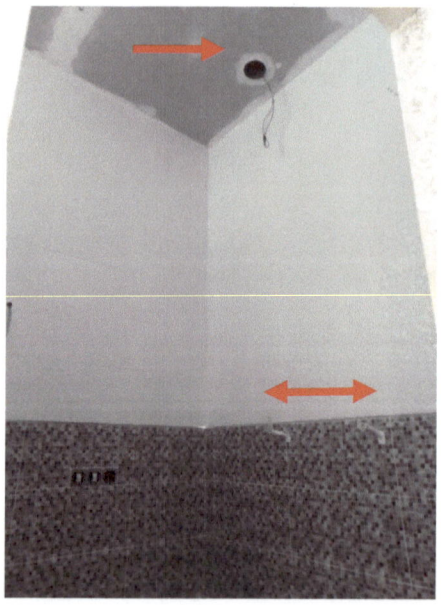

Figure 3. We can observe: forced-ventilation circuit and other circuit to wait for the heating-towel rail.

2. FUNCTION OF THE BATHS AND KITCHENS ON A CONVENTIONAL HOUSE

The spaces of a home or a local could be divided in:

- The ones that include machines as the oven or the cooker on a kitchen or constituents or taps on a bath.

- The ones called "rooms" where can be or not, but as a priority, not.

As I said before, this zones or locals are submitted to the daily functional use of the inhabitants.

2.1. THE KITCHEN AND THE LAUNDRY

The kitchen and the laundry are the zones where are ubicated the majority of machines, you should install the adient potence of electricity on the house or flat to the basic standards of oven-cooker, dish-washing machine, clothes-washing machine, extractor and the heater.

In the kitchen, you put into storage aliments and wash them and the dishes...and even if you have an office you also eat there.

In the laundry, you can even place the heater, wahs the clothes yoursef and install a frame for drying clothes. Anyway, it serves too to storage cleaning products.

By the way, I'll show you three examples of solutions: one with the laundry non-vinculated to the kitchen, another vinculated and finally one kitchen without laundry and a litlle office.

- **Example 1**

On this flat, you can observe into the central zone of kitchen and bath, the laundry with its storage of cleaning products. This is non-vinculated to the kitchen and the acces to that room is annex thanks to the corridor, minimizing circulations of the users into the flat.

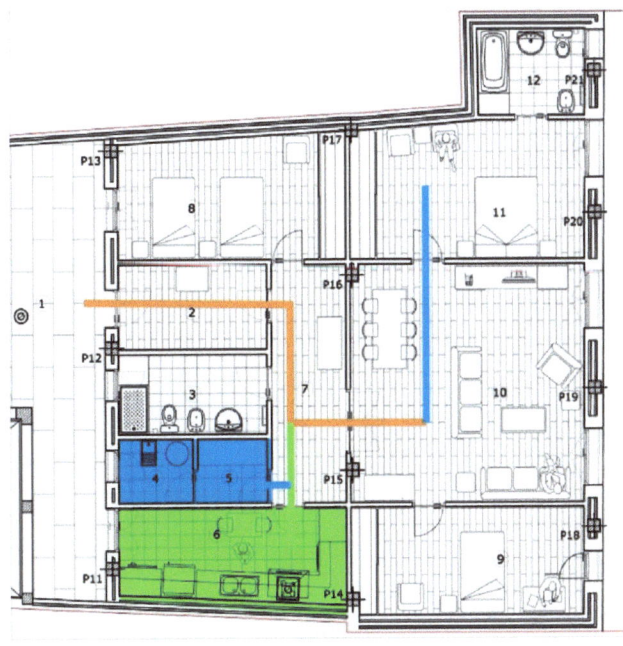

Figure 4. Zones and circulation by privacity.

- **Example 2**

In the semi-public zone of the first floor level on the Figure 1, we observe a laundry vinculated to the kitchen and its office. The laundry here, goes nowhere and it is a residual place, except to enter to the patio, to dry the clothes. On this case, the heater is ubicated in the laundry.

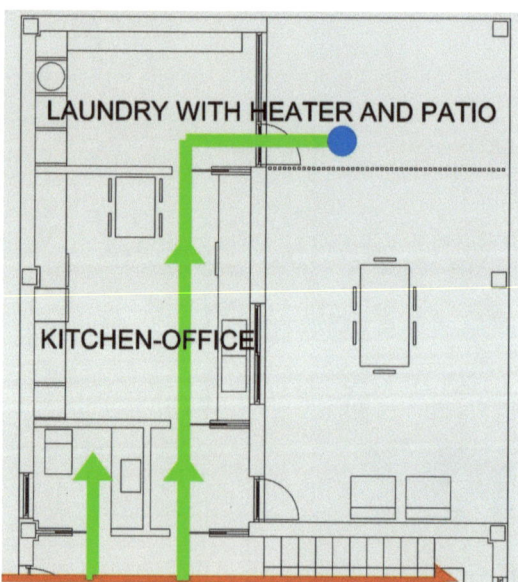

Figure 5. The laundry and the patio as a private zone.

- **Example 3**

This is a typical case of kitchen with office and with a heater of natural gas integrated on the zone.

As you can observe in the photos taken of the construction of a rehabilitation of a flat, we have all the connections to the machines, you cal also see the canalization of the conducts of heating and extractor units.

Figure 6. Connectios and tubes of gases extraction.

Figure 7. Office and zonification.

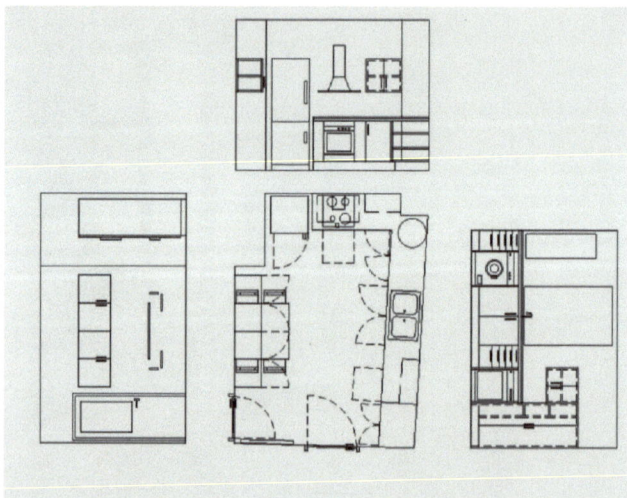

Figure 8. Design of the furniture of the kitchen.

2.2. THE SUITTE

The suitte is an architectonical resort coming from hotels and adapted to the houses of today. They are very common on houses or flats of whealty people, who promote them, so they aren't very much seen.

I offer you two examples. On the first one, the bath can be used by two person – matrimony- by the same time. The second one is a typicall suitte.

- **Example 1**

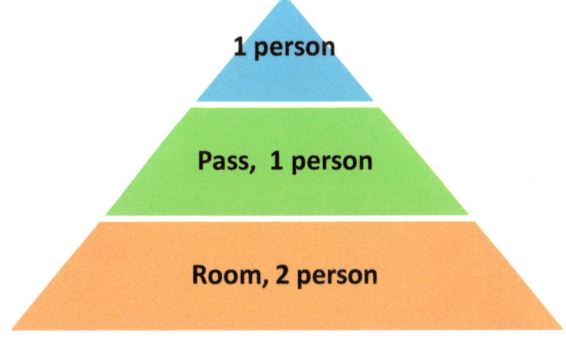

Figura 9. Hierarchy of use.

As you see the colours of the diagram of the Figure 9 , we understand that the room is ocupated ba two people. In the first room of the bath, we place the washbasin and is a zone of trespassing to the   shower,   bidet   or   WC.

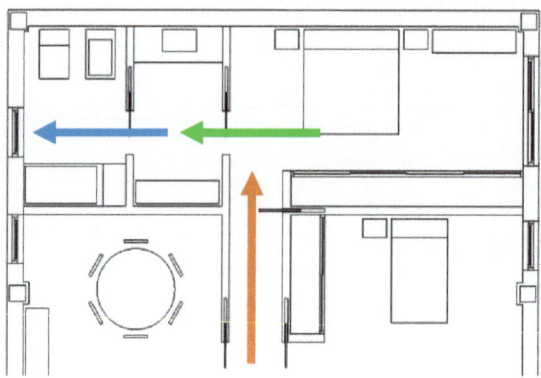

Figure 10. Hierarchy of use, diagram on a plan.

- **Example 2**

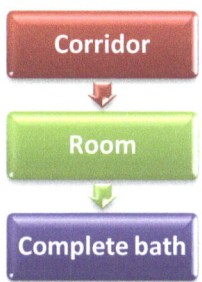

Figure 11. Detail of a conventional suitte.

In this case, there is no built-in wardrobe, but the corridor at the entrance of the suitte allows to place a wardrobe in front of the bath.

2.3. THE BATH OF COMMON USE

In the room of a bath, you can find:

- Washbasin
- Shower / Bathtube
- Bidet
- Urinary (optional)
- WC
- Laundry (optional)
- Mirror
- Furniture
- Accesories
- Partitions / curtains
- Heating units

Here you can smarten yourself up, but a bath has to be prepared to the evacuation of human refuses.

As the number of occupants, I'll show two examples:

- **Example 1**

  High occupation:

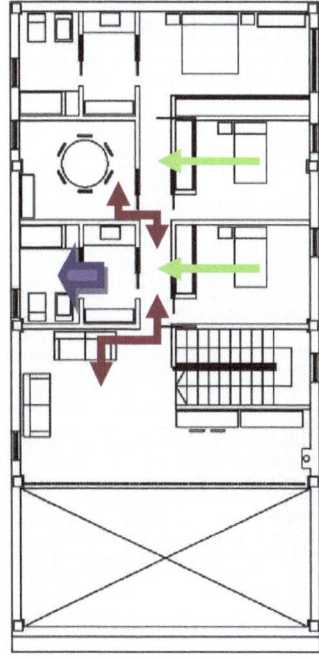

Figure 11. General bath of a house of high occupation.

Because of being several bedromms and another rooms, the house has a high capacity. You can acceed from the corridor and it can be used by two occupants, one of them having a bath and another washing his or her teeths, for example.

- **Ejemplo 2**
  Conventional flat:

Figure 12. General bath of a conventional flat.

Figure 12 shows a complete bath with a window to a patio that allows enter luminosity and fresh air. The owners prefer place the laundry here because it is big and place a frame for drying clothes.

3. THE MINIMUM HOUSE OR FLAT

The projects and studies of a minimum house –even agrupations of them- come from the second CIAM congress at the year 1929 until today. They obey to political movements because of the necesity in a lot of countries of a cheap and accessible living.

Here, the function doesn't change on baths and kitchens but there is a minor number of machines because we count with less space.

In such a little flats is primordial to study the circulations between the rooms, kitchens and baths and even inside them.

This flats or houses need a detailed and minucious study.

3.1. Cases

This plans are several School exercises at the Superior and Technical School of Architecture in Barcelona, where I studied my degree.

They show you two minimum flats or apartments.

At the image, I paint the secuences in the kitchen as follows:

1. Take the lunch or dinner from the fridge
2. Wash the meal
3. Cook it
4. Serve it

With blue colour, the directions to go to the bath if the users are in the living or at the bedroom.

With red colour the movemements they make to prepare the meal and serve it.

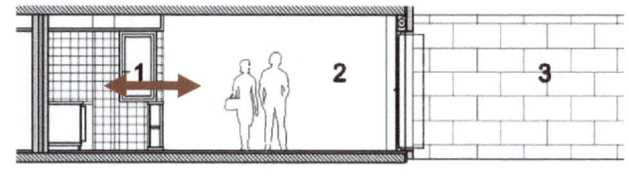

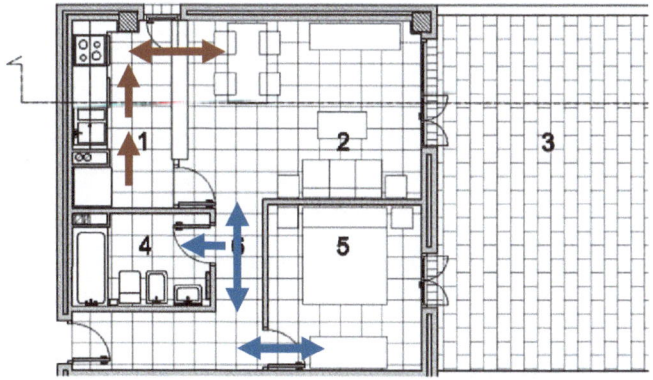

Figure 13. Minimum flat of 50 m2.

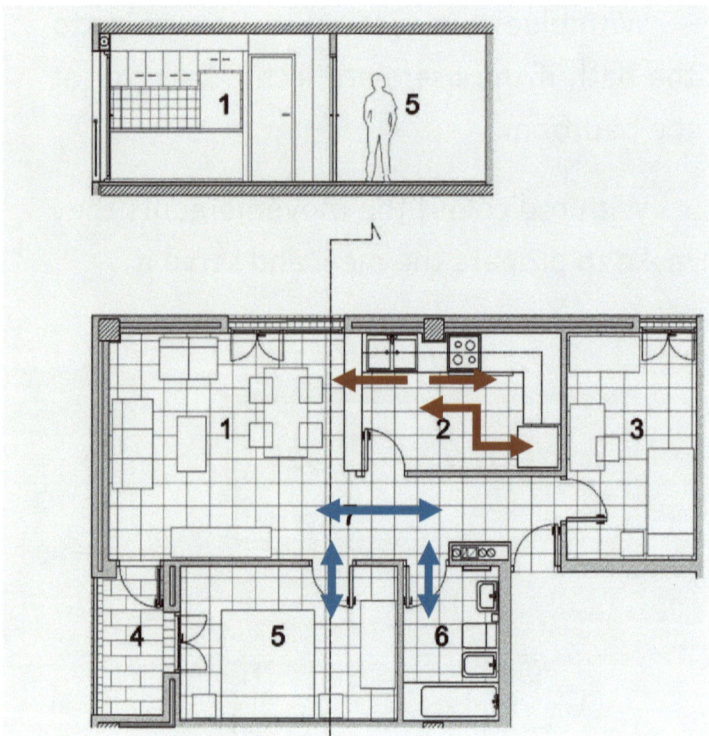

Figure 14. Minimum flat of 65 m2.

Finally, I'll show a details of the same flats exposed before. They are details of the kitchen and the bath and you can see that the machines in the kitchen are the minimum even the baths are complete with teir accessories and space for the heating units in the rear or next to the door.

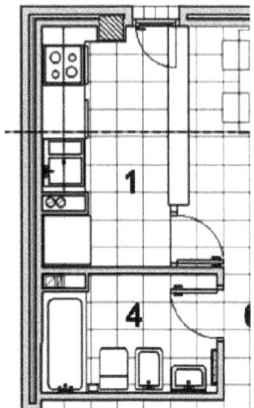

Detail of Figure 13

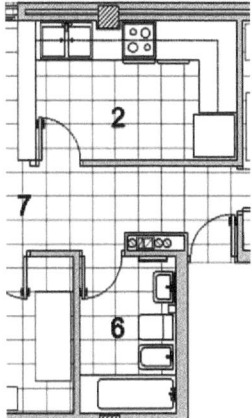

Detail of Figure 14

5. EPILOGUE

I conclude this monograh that in a big features pretends systematize and give to the lector some rules to design and place baths and kitchens on a house or flat.

This booklet analyzes some cases, so you can take them as reference all the times you want or it can serve as way of inspiration to project or create an architectural work as the clients' desire.

The examples are taken from my experience at work, visits or school exercises, so they are confident to the lector and verificated by the years in each case.

I am grateful because your time on reading this booklet and thanks a lot!